HistoryCaps Presents:

Spies of the American Revolution

*The History of George Washington's Secret Spying Ring
(The Culper Ring)*

By Howard Brinkley

Bookcaps™ Study Guides

www.bookcaps.com

HOWARD BRINKLEY

Spies of the American Revolution

Copyright © 2012 by Golgotha Press, Inc.

Printed in the United States of America

Table of Contents

ABOUT HISTORYCAPS

HistoryCaps is an imprint of BookCaps™ Study Guides. With each book, a brief period of history is recapped. We publish a wide array of topics (from baseball and music to science and philosophy), so check our growing catalogue regularly (www.book-caps.com) to see our newest books.

CHAPTER 1: A CITY UNDER SIEGE

In the summer of 1776, the future of the American colonies was delicately balanced between an uncertain independence and continued rule by the British Crown. The first salvos of war were fired in Boston, but the climate of fear and mistrust quickly spread throughout the colonies. With neighbor pitted against neighbor, acts of terrible cruelty and injustice were commonplace.

After their embarrassing defeat at Boston, Britain's commanders needed a new base of operations. From a military perspective, the city of New York, chosen by the rebels as their national capital, had enormous strategic value. It had a marvelous harbor, was easy to defend, and Long Island could theoretically provide provisions should supply lines from the Mother Country be interrupted. It was no secret, then, that the British had their eye on the port of New York.

Long Island was a stronghold of Loyalists, or Tories – Citizens who sided with the British monarchy. The island, therefore, made a perfect staging area for the eventual attack on Brooklyn and Manhattan. As the rebels consolidated their power in Massachusetts, Connecticut and Pennsylvania, Tory refugees came across Long Island Sound in sizeable numbers. Meanwhile, any rebel sympathizers living on the island had to keep a low profile or risk being harassed or imprisoned. Those who fled to Connecticut almost certainly had their property razed, and their goods seized.

For his part, General George Washington understood that the more the British entrenched themselves in New York, the weaker their claim to the rest of the Colonies became, especially in the interior. He also saw the need for current, actionable information on what exactly the British Army and Navy were doing in the city. Were they gearing up for a spring campaign? Building fortifications for an extended siege? Were re-enforcements on the way? A successful defense, much less a vigorous attack strategy, could not be carried out by the Continental Army without answers to these questions. But getting that information would not be easy.

Before the British seized the island of Manhattan, Washington made a vain attempt to learn more about British troop movements. He requested that two of his generals, William Heath and George Clinton, begin setting up an intelligence corridor between Long Island and Connecticut. In a letter to Heath, Washington talks about the need to "meet the enemy" before they settle in to comfortably. "Doing that will require early and accurate intelligence of troop strengths, movements, and so on." Heath and Clinton are cooperative, but, in fact, have little experience in the kind of operation that Washington envisions. No one in the 18th century, for that matter, had yet developed any strong ideas about what military espionage could mean in the big picture.

Washington had strictly military intelligence on his mind – raw data about the enemy's numbers and plans. He had performed just that sort of work during the French and Indian War, when he was a strapping young officer looking for glory. The problem lay in the fact that no real system existed for gathering this kind of tactical information, and the complexities of the Revolutionary War situation were new territory for all involved. The civilian population was restless and fearful, while ordinary soldiers didn't have the skills needed for proper spy work.

Not surprisingly, the first attempt to gather intelligence from the British-held areas of Long Island was not a rousing success. General Clinton managed to recruit two willing and able young men – Benjamin Ludlum and William Treadwell – to cross the Long Island Sound in secret, but the results were useless. With no training on how to do their jobs and what to look for behind enemy lines, the pair reported mostly exaggerated or pointless trivia. Washington was disappointed and worried that no superior intelligence would ever come out of the city, a reality that would seal the doom of his army.

What more confirmation of that doom did Washington need than the takeover of Manhattan, which the British completed in a total rout on September 15, 1776? The Continental Army was running scared.

*   *   *

As the British were forcing the rebels out of Manhattan, young Nathan Hale was heading blindly toward his death on Long Island. He had been commissioned by George Washington to gather first-hand intelligence of British troop movements:

"Learn what you can, but blend in. You can't risk capture. We have to know when the British plan to strike, and with what forces." It was part of a last-ditch, failed effort to defend against the inevitable British invasion of Manhattan. With no formal training as a spy, he was an easy mark. Robert Rogers, a cutthroat veteran of the French and Indian War, captured Hale with little fanfare. General Howe signed the death warrant, and the British let Hale's stiff corpse swing in the breeze for a few days as a warning to rebel sympathizers. It was a grim reminder of the dangers of spying, and a logical reason for sensible men and women to avoid the occupation.

"We can't depend on amateurs for this kind of business," said Washington, when he learned of Hale's execution. "Even if young Mr. Hale had not been captured, I don't know that any information would have stopped Howe's attack."

Privately, Washington considered the idea of commissioning civilians to do the "dirty work" of spying. There were obvious advantages and disadvantages to the plan. For the strategically minded general, the biggest argument in favor of the idea was simply that it had never been tried.

CHAPTER 2: A TURNING POINT

The failures of Hale, Ludlum and Treadwell were on General Washington's mind as he spent the winter of '76–'77 in the woods near Morristown, New Jersey. The commander-in-chief of the ragtag Continental Army shifted uneasily on his seat, considering how to overcome the superior numbers of the entrenched British forces. For nearly a year, the war against the Mother Country had consisted of one defeat after another, and his staff was losing faith. They had abandoned New York City, escaping in the dead of night by the skin of their teeth. General

Cornwallis had chased and hounded them through the woods of New Jersey and Pennsylvania. The British seemed always one step ahead of them. At any point, General Howe could have dealt the crushing blow; to this day, no one knows why he didn't. For his part, Washington was at his wit's end. Spending the winter in the cold wilderness with another summer of embarrassing defeats on the horizon was not an appealing thought. The war had never felt so hopeless.

"We know nothing of what the Redcoats are doing. Where is General Howe? What's his plan? Will he stay in New York, or move on Philadelphia?" These thoughts kept the general awake at night, planning, scheming, and working through contingency scenarios. What he lacked was information to make the best decisions. Battlefields are messy, confused places, but the situation near the end of 1776 was especially daunting.

Washington's advisors had no answers. Many of his generals had no faith in his command ability. His senior commanders, Nathanial Greene and Horatio Gates among them, had performed admirably in avoiding defeat. Boston and much of the rest of New England were firmly in the hands of the Revolutionaries. The countryside, where most of the people lived, was strongly in favor of independence. However, the British still held a military advantage, especially in terms of their navy. Canada to the north, and the vast open expanse of the Atlantic Ocean to the east were friendly territory for the Redcoats. Washington knew that creativity, luck and some friendly help were needed to turn the tide.

*   *   *

"We have to keep the Redcoats on their toes," said Washington. "I have a plan; it may not work. But if it does, we could seriously boost morale, and let the British know that there's still fight in us. It's what we need right now, more than food or boots. We need something to change our prospects."

One of his advisors piped up. "Sir, the men's enlistments are expiring. The army is dwindling. We have, I think, fewer than 2,000 soldiers fit for duty."

"All the more reason to move quickly, decisively, right now. We need action."

"But sir," his advisor complained, "It's December, and snowing, and the river is ice-jammed."

"Anything worth doing is difficult. If it were easy, we might have already won this war. Prepare for a crossing – McKonkey's Ferry – and get me Colonel Knox."

One of the commander-in-chief's closest confidantes, Colonel Henry Knox, was a stout but gentlemanly soldier with a razor-sharp intellect. Before the war broke out, he owned a bookstore and dabbled in military history. In many ways, war was his "calling." It was the proving ground where his immense knowledge was put to practical use.

Knox ambled into the general's tent like a bloated but well-mannered pack animal, and fixed his bright, beady eyes on Washington.

"You've got a plan, I see - a plan to cross the river? I thought so. It's just the thing we need right now."

"How is it you always know what I'm thinking? You probably considered this before I did," said Washington.

"It's my duty to know your mind and put your thoughts into action. It's why I'm here."

Washington flashed a wry smile at Knox. "Listen – My agent Mr. Honeyman has made a report on the enemy troops in Trenton. He estimates only 1,000 or so Hessian mercenaries. They'll make an easy quarry, and the gunpowder and provisions will be useful. We'll move on the day after Christmas. They won't be expecting us, I imagine."

"Let's work out the details," said Knox, "because crossing a river with 2,000 men is no small feat. This Mr. Honeyman, he must be very skilled at his duty."

"He's the most skilled that I know of; If I could have ten like him, we could win the war inside of a month, I imagine. But that's just the trouble. There are so few who have a natural affinity for spying and scouting. It takes real courage."

Washington smiled and regarded the stained map of the Delaware River and the British deployments. Together, he and Knox finalized the logistics of a decisive surprise attack on Hessian troops in Trenton. It was the first small step toward altering the balance of power in the war. If nothing else, the victory in Trenton verified the importance of intelligence.

*   *   *

Colonel John Cadwalader was the sly, crafty sort of commander who performed well in the service of his superior, General Washington. He was forward thinking in his approach to battlefield espionage. As the rebel army's numbers were dwindling – there were maybe 3,000 left out of an original 20,000 – Cadwalader dispatched an anonymous but clearly well-qualified civilian to sow misinformation among the British officers. It was a success. The British believed that Washington's army was still a match for them, even when it was nowhere close. Cadwalader's espionage was modest, but it may have stalled a more decisive move by the enemy. At any rate, the colonel's bold move of using a civilian agent let Washington know that such a strategy was not only possible, but could be pulled off with satisfactory results. Only two things were necessary: a stable base of operations, and reliable agents who could cross enemy lines without arousing suspicion.

CHAPTER 3: LAYING THE GROUNDWORK

Nathaniel Sackett was firmly convinced of the need for revolution and a new government with local representation. At the risk of his own wellbeing, he had thrown all his support behind the revolutionary cause. A middle-aged and successful gentleman, Sackett was nevertheless surprised to receive a letter from none other than George Washington. As a member of New York's Committee for Detecting and Defeating Conspiracies, he had rubbed elbows with prominent people before. But the commander in chief of the army? This was new territory. Sack-

ett studied the letter with care: "On the recommen-
dation of your colleague Mr. William Duer, I am
requesting that you assist the efforts of our military
by undertaking a ultra secret, very dangerous, but
immensely critical mission. Namely, we desperately
need early intelligence on the British situation in
Manhattan." Sackett felt a thrill of excitement, and
not a little fear, at the thought of being an agent in
the cause for righteousness. "Our efforts so far in
the area of spying have been less than ideal. What
we need is a system in place for funneling information out of Manhattan on something like a regular
basis. To that end, I am prepared to commission
you on a salary of 50 dollars per month. Also at
your disposal you will have a cash fund of 500 dollars. Should you need some other form of currency,
that can be arranged, as well. Hire whomever you
feel is qualified and necessary to complete the mission."

Washington knew he was putting a lot of trust in a
civilian. He also knew that cooperation form the
military would be necessary to ensure success. "I
can't have the bruised ego of field commanders in-
terfering with this mission. Sackett needs a military
liaison," Washington thought to himself. As dis-
cretely as possible, the commander in chief selected
a young captain by the name of Benjamin Tallmadge to serve as Sackett's military contact. Tallmadge was an up-and-comer, and Washington saw

for him a bright future. He was well connected to powerful people in New England. He had resisted joining the army until 1776, having a cautious streak rather than the hotheadedness of his peers. He was close friends, in fact, with Nathan Hale. During the evacuation of Brooklyn, his brother William was captured by the British and placed on one of the deadly prison ships, where he died of neglect. The combined loss of his brother and Hale made a deep impression on Tallmadge. No longer was he moderate in his feelings against the Crown. After New York, he was ready to do anything in the service of his commander.

Tallmadge and his men stayed behind after the loss of Manhattan, guarding the east side of the Hudson River against possible British movements. Eventually, the regiment settled in to Connecticut. Tallmadge was a captain in the Second Dragoons – a kind of 18th-century Special Forces unit, complete with dashing uniforms and metal helmets. For much of 1777, the captain served two masters. Within his regiment, he answered to Colonel Elisha Sheldon. His other job, conducted as secretly as possible, was to help rebel spies get back and forth across Long Island Sound.

*   *   *

Major John Clark presented himself before Captain
Tallmadge in January 1777, looking every bit like the
stocky, confident lawyer turned soldier he was re-
puted to be. Clark was chosen as the first agent to
cross over to Long Island and assess the situation.

Tallmadge looked the agent up and down, wonder-
ing if this half-crazy mission would mean death
just as it had for Hale. The British held a tight grip
on the island and all the waterways surrounding it.
On the other hand, he thought, this soldier has talents that Hale lacked, not to mention battle-tested
wits and experience. Plus, Tallmadge could provide
him with advice and resources for navigating
through the local population. After all, he was a native of Setauket, a small village on the eastern end
of the island.

"Listen, Major," began Tallmadge, "I have sent word
ahead to some terrifically particular friends in my
hometown. There, you'll find a warm place to sleep,
and food to keep you in top shape. Setauket is a
town friendly to our cause; my father is a minister
in the town."

"Is that so?" remarked the affable Clark. "What de-
nomination, then?"

"Presbyterian. *Strongly* Presbyterian."

"Ah, so you've got fire in your blood? You Presbyterians make excellent rebels – excellent prosecutors, too, I might add."

"I'll take that as a compliment. But I would argue the point about 'fire in my blood.' I'm not half so fiery as my father, nor so much as my poor dead brother. But this war may be lighting a fuse in me. Still, I want to be as careful as possible in the execution of this mission. Everything depends on it. If you're successful, then we'll have an avenue into the heart of British occupied territory. And that's the first step in getting them out."

Clark studied the young captain carefully, as if he were a witness on trial. "Do you have any particular recommendations? What's your experience in this sort of business?"

"I may be a Dragoon," responded Tallmadge, "but I'm not above doing whatever is necessary. Spy work, done properly, is as honorable as any other military endeavor. As for advice, I'll give you just this much: Keep a low profile. Trust absolutely no one. Carry nothing on your person that indicates your allegiances. Setauket is your only place of refuge. I'll give you the names and locales of prominent citizens in the community. Now, let us work on a cover story. You have to have a *reason* for being on Long Island, after all."

*　　*　　*

History doesn't record what Major Clark did between January and September 1777. Even in his autobiography, he carefully omitted his activities during this period. It's probable that he was making frequent, daring explorations of British-held territory. With the help of Tallmadge's friends and relations, Clark managed never to draw undue attention on himself.

In April, Tallmadge was promoted and recalled to New Jersey. In his absence, Nathanial Sackett managed the spy network on his own. He excelled at the work. In his letters to Washington, he frequently discussed new ideas and techniques for maximizing the usable information that could be pulled out of enemy territory. One of his ideas would prove to be the genesis of the Culper Ring – America's first truly effective spy network.

Sackett explained that his spies' tactical missions weren't delivering enough information. "New York is not a battlefield as such, General, and we have to consider a new approach. I have given the matter much thought. I believe what we need now is a sort of 'stationary agent,' someone who can blend in seamlessly, all the time gathering news of the situation. We'll of course still need agents who can move back and forth, delivering regular reports and the like. I still have many particulars to work out. I understand that you might think the work is unseemly, or perhaps too risky. I admit that there will be considerable risk for anyone who undertakes this kind of 'hiding in plain sight.' Even now, I'm looking for the sort of people who might excel at this role."

Ambitious would barely describe what Sackett imagined. In his first test of the new strategy, he stationed an agent in Manhattan posing as a poultry trader. With its thriving black market, it was easy to blend in as an ordinary business person. It was less easy, however, to get truly usable information. Sackett quickly found an answer: He found someone who was already well acquainted with the Tory leadership in New York. This gave him the idea of getting agents close to the center of power. The strategy was a revolution in spycraft.

In yet another remarkable mission, he sent the wife of a rebel to General Howe himself to complain about the plundering of her grain stores by rebel forces. The British never once suspected that the woman might be an agent. They talked freely of their plans in front of her. The information she returned was both valuable and timely.

Sackett didn't remain in the spy business, but his contributions were enormous. He had implanted in

Washington the idea of agents "setting up shop" behind the lines. Likewise, he had impressed upon the general the importance of getting intelligence quickly, as well as gathering multiple reports on the same event for the purposes of cross-referencing. Sackett's lessons would be vitally beneficial when Washington founded the Culper Ring shortly thereafter.

CHAPTER 4: ATTACK AND COUNTERATTACK

After the loss of New York, the battlefield of the Revolutionary War became an uncertain, unpredictable place for the rebels. The British held superiority in numbers and appeared to be on a path to total victory. Constantly chased through the wilderness, Washington was unable to glean any useful intelligence from his scouts. He was reacting rather than acting. Deserters from the enemy ranks, a frequent source of information, were nonexistent. Why leave the side of victory, after all?

The British, for their part, put into motion a plan that they hoped would bring the war to a swift conclusion. With spring giving way to summer, the Canadian segment of the British Army was prepared to move south and cut New England off from the rest of the colonies. In theory, General John Burgoyne was to join Sir Henry Clinton's army in Albany, thereby controlling the whole Hudson River valley. Meanwhile, General Howe would bring forces north from New York. In the end, the plan was just too complicated for its time. Miscommunication, indecisive leadership, and harassing attacks from stealthy rebels slowed down the northern armies. The entire plan fell apart.

Howe believed, with good reason, that Philadelphia was a more critical target than the Hudson valley. He went south instead of north, well aware that he was abandoning thousands of British soldiers in upper New York. As a result, Burgoyne's entire army was lost, and the British were dealt a significant blow. It was the first and last time they would attempt an attack from the north. Still, they had New York. So long as they did, it was difficult to imagine how the revolution could end in victory.

Ever since the British had stormed Brooklyn and Manhattan Island in late summer, 1776, the bustling port city had been held under a spell. Soldiers filled the streets and public houses. A wartime mentality had permeated the city, yet the fighting was, in fact, far away. The few remaining citizens had to play both sides of the war just to keep food on their tables. A thriving black market developed, which military leadership deliberately ignored – General Howe accepted it as an unavoidable reality of war. The British, overall, were in a ticklish position. There was no doubt a substantial military advantage in holding New York City. It was a convenient launching point for attacks up and down the coast. However, the trouble lay in extending and consolidating that power. Howe knew that the war could end in stalemate if he simply held on to a single city indefinitely, no matter how strategically valuable. With that in mind, Howe set out for Philadelphia in September, 1777. He hoped to capture the rebel Congress, effectively beheading the revolution and sacking its capital (again).

The move to annex Philadelphia was a mixed success. Washington was unable to block Howe's progress. At the battle of Brandywine Creek, Howe again outfoxed Washington. The commander in chief was driven from the battlefield with more than 2,000 casualties. He blamed poor intelligence for the rout. The city fell, but Congress and many of the citizens had already fled. Sackett's New York spy network had paid dividends, providing advance knowledge about Howe's movements. Rather than consolidating power, the British general's gambit had spread his forces thinner. He could do nothing but settle in for the winter. Another summer of campaigns had come and gone. The lines on the map had shifted relatively little, and the outcome of the war was still hugely unclear. As the purely military aspect of the war stagnated, espionage would become more salient.

*　　*　　*

Major John Clark was brought down from Long Island to conduct a new spy network in and around Philadelphia. He had become so skilled at his job that the names and activities of his agents are all lost to history. It is known that he moved constantly, always fearing detection from locals or British scouts. Clark's excellent work won high praise from Washington. The two corresponded frequently by letter. Of course, they never used their real names and cleverly concealed the "actual" message of the communication. This was a typical strategy in the early days of military intelligence. Washington needed reminding once or twice before learning the critical importance of secrecy.

One of Clark's favorite tricks was to feed misleading information to General Howe. Washington provided the misinformation, and one of Clark's trusted double agents delivered it. Thanks to this campaign, Howe never had a clear idea of where the rebel general was going, or how many soldiers were under his command. Many of Clark's agents were caught and probably came to a bad end in the hands of the British. However, the major was always able to find adequate replacements. He seems to have developed a kind of training regimen for his new recruits.

By the spring of 1778, Clark had retired from the spy trade because of poor health. He was given a desk job as an auditor. The British made changes, too. Sir William Howe resigned as commander of Her Majesty's forces. Henry Clinton took his place, and chose to leave Philadelphia. The city was too difficult to supply, and the British forces were spread way too thin. Clinton, therefore, retreated to New York.

Washington spoke with his aides about the need for someone to fill Clark's role. "He was the best at his work that anyone could ask for – all his reports were accurate and timely, not one bit of trivial information. How are we going to replace him?"

"Sir, we could train a man in his techniques. He's left us with much knowledge."

"Yes, sure, there are techniques, but Clark had an instinct. That cannot be taught."

"New York is a big place, general. I'm sure there are qualified people in the area. What about Tallmadge of the Dragoons? He's done work like that before, and done it well."

Washington closed his eyes, lost in thought. After what seemed like a long time, he said, "Tallmadge is a good idea, but we need to go further. The network has to be larger, with more eyes and ears on the ground. If we're going to put the squeeze on the redcoats, we have to know what their plans the instant they're laid out."

Just then, a courier arrived with a letter. The author was Lieutenant Caleb Brewster. Washington had never heard of him, but the contents fascinated him: "I am stationed now in Norwalk, on the Connecticut side of the Sound. My position gives me access to Long Island. I know of several ways to safely get onto the island and back across without detection. I would like to offer my services to that end."

Washington was intrigued, but cautious. He didn't know what to make of a volunteer spy, and only a lieutenant at that. He sent a straightforward reply: "My dear Mr. Brewster, I have attempted to set up a permanent spy network since the beginning of the revolution. Sadly, I have suffered more failures than successes. Let me tell you what the successful spies had in common: they did not exaggerate troop numbers; they knew the difference between essential information and trivia; they maintained layers upon layers of secrecy; they had the courage of lions; most of all, they didn't get caught. Can I rely upon you for these things at the very least? I look forward to your answer. If you prove worthy, we will certainly spare no expense to see that your work is carried out."

*   *   *

Caleb Brewster was an imposing figure. He had a sense of humor, a big laugh, and courage to spare. People often underestimated his intelligence. He was intelligent enough to see that Washington needed help in the form of ground truth about the British military situation. Unlike Benjamin Tallmadge, Brewster had no specific grudge against the British. He seemed to love action and fighting for its own sake, so the war was a time of high excitement for him. He also seemed to relish the idea of being part of the spy trade, something most soldiers gladly steered clear of.

On August 27, 1778, Brewster sent Washington his first of many intelligence reports to his commander in chief. He provided accounts of British ship movements and troop redeployments. The most valuable piece of news was that the British were sending reinforcements to Newport, Rhode Island. Washington was duly impressed, but realized that one man did not a spy network make. There would need to be more agents, and Brewster needed help to become even better at his task. The Culper Ring was beginning to take shape.

CHAPTER 5: THE RING EXPANDS

Espionage during the Revolutionary War was an imperfect, often improvised art form. The basic tactics were the same on both sides of the battlefield. Agents adopted false names and never carried incriminating evidence on their persons. Messages were either memorized or transmitted in code. Sometimes, a messaged would be encased in a small steel ball, which could be swallowed if necessary. But the means of gathering the information changed dramatically between the start of the war and its end.

Through trial and error, Washington came to an understanding of what made for a good spy. The most vital trait was intelligence, he discovered. To keep his or her neck out of the noose, a spy had to plan ahead and be resourceful. In its own way, spying was every bit as dangerous as infantry fighting. The biggest difference, of course, was that captured spies suffered an inglorious, anonymous death. Ironically, a terrific spy also had to have a high level of integrity and honesty. Washington learned the hard way that amateur spies often delivered overblown reports rather than having nothing to report. These inaccurate reports were, in fact, more damaging than no report at all.

Washington realized early in the war that two logistical factors were necessary to guarantee an effective spy network: a stable base of operations, and multiple agents spread throughout enemy territory. Likewise, a dependable channel of communications was essential to ensure that information made it across the lines in time to be useful. It wasn't until 1778, after the British had retrenched in New York, that all of these factors came together.

*   *   *

Washington selected General Charles Scott to head up the new intelligence network, which at that point consisted only of Caleb Brewster. He also contacted Major Tallmadge, directing him to help Scott recruit agents and set up lines of communication. Tallmadge had gained a wealth of experience while working with Sackett and Clark. For his part, Scott hated his new responsibilities. "I am suspicious of spies – their information is vague and most often useless," he complained to Washington. "It's a despicable practice. I have much more important things to do."

Washington was understandably annoyed. "We have a great responsibility before us, of bringing the Revolution to its conclusion. Regardless of your personal feelings, intelligence of the enemy is more crucial now than ever before. We have them pinned. The French failed to blockade the sea; our only avenue is to learn all we can of the British plans. This means spying. I am urging you to work more diligently to set up an apparatus that will shed light on the goings-on in the British-held territories of Manhattan Island and Long Island. Delegate as much of your field work to subordinates as possible. The spy network is the critical thing just now. I cannot stress that enough."

Washington's pleading fell on deaf ears. As it happened, the bulk of the responsibilities fell upon

Major Tallmadge, which wasn't entirely a bad thing. He immediately identified a promising candidate for the work of spycraft. Abraham Woodhull, a Long Island farmer and black market privateer, had the good sense, caution, and skills of observation to make an excellent agent. Tallmadge summoned him for an interview.

"So, you were a farmer before the fighting?" began the major.

"Yes, sir, and still am," replied the quiet and polite Woodhull.

"Farming is an honorable occupation, to be sure. But surely you know that trading British goods for British money is illegal?"

"I, ah ... but you see, the family ... times are tough, and ... The trading helps us stay afloat, keep the farm supplied, and ..." Woodhull was visibly nervous. After previously spending time in jail for smuggling, he feared worse things to come.

"It's alright Abraham, I understand. I'm not here to send you back to jail. In fact, I'm here to propose a job for you. We know you have experience crossing the Sound without detection. Even when you are detected, you look like a part of the scenery, so to speak. You're a native. In short, you're exactly the sort of person we need for some – I'll not lie –

dangerous work we're undertaking. By 'we' I mean the Continental Army. Do you understand so far?"

"Yes, I believe so. So the charges against me ..."

"Don't worry about a thing. General Washington has heard about your boatmanship and knack for keeping a low profile. If you can move goods across the water, you can just as easily move information. What say you to that?" Tallmadge smiled, obviously excited to find such a talented candidate for the spy trade.

"Anything I might do to further the Revolution, I will do."

"Good. There's just one small catch. I know that the profits of trading are tempting. Can you assure me that you'll dedicate most of your energy to the information trade, only keeping up the goods trade as absolutely necessary."

"I can promise you that. Have no fear."

Washington was highly pleased to learn of Woodhull. But, for safety's sake, they did not meet in person. Should a spy be captured, it was vital that he have little or no knowledge of commanders' locations and plans. Communication, therefore, consisted of a chain of middlemen, no one of them "knowing too much."

Later, Tallmadge chose aliases for himself and Woodhull. He became "John Bolton." Abraham Woodhull took the name of "Samuel Culper." Samuel was the name of Tallmadge's younger brother. Culper was a shortened version of "Culpeper," the Virginia county in which Washington had been a surveyor as a youth. Caleb Brewster refused to take an alias, saying, "I will not skulk around under a fake name like some low-life." And so Brewster signed all of his letters with his own name in giant letters. It was just the kind of person he was, bold to a fault.

*   *   *

In the early days of the Culper Ring, General Scott called all the shots. From his perspective, military intelligence was less serious than battlefield tactics. He shortchanged the spy operation and continually undermined his subordinate, Tallmadge. Scott's strategy was the method of failure: individual scouting missions with little chance of success. Even when agents returned alive, they were unable to glean darned much useful information. Under the old, uninspired system of reconnaissance, there was precious little return on investment. Scott knew that Tallmadge was one of Washington's favorites; this may explain much of his actions. He was known to be jealous and vindictive. Fortunately, the commander in chief eventually saw that the traditional approach was failing. Tallmadge was ready to step in and offer a compelling, but risky alternative.

"General, I have worked close with both Mr. Sackett and Major Clark. I have learned a vast deal about the spy game. I would like to propose an ambitious plan. Here, is what we know: The British aren't going anywhere. We have them fully surrounded in New York. What's called for now is an embedded network of agents and a line of communication out of the city. These forays have given us nothing. Just recently, three of five agents were caught at British checkpoints. We can only imagine what' happened to them."

"I understand your concerns, and agree that what we have tried so far simply isn't working," Washington tells Tallmadge. "This is a unique situation, demanding a unique approach. I am curious to hear the details of what you suggest."

"Very well, sir. We know from experience that run-of-the-mill scouts and spies often report inflated numbers, or tell outlandish tales. An empty report is seen as failure, so many just make things up. I believe an embedded presence will quash those tendencies and offer better outcomes in the long run. I've had the happy fortune to encounter many able-bodied and clever men this season, not the least of them Mr. 'Culper.'"

"Major, the key, I think, is this: We must turn the advantage of holding New York from an advantage to a disadvantage. Does your plan effect that end?" enquired the still uncertain Washington.

"I could not agree more with your military assessment. With the bulk of His Majesty's forces are concentrated in the city, we have an incredible opportunity. What they see as a strength, we can exploit as a weakness. There's only one obstacle at this time. General Scott seeks to undermine all that I do and say. He is dedicated to the old ways, the kind of thinking that led poor Nathan Hale to the gallows. Battlefield scout techniques just won't help us here. We need *minute* details, General."

"I would be lying if I told you I didn't think it was ludicrous. The complexities, the cost, and the risks are all enormous. But maybe it's exactly the right idea. I'm willing to try. God knows we need to build on our momentum. A knockout punch would be just the thing. If they're not harassed in some way, the British can stay on that rotten island until the end of days – and we'll never be truly independent, not with a parasitic leech sucking the blood from our land."

By October of 1778, Scott had been quietly taken out of the loop. Tallmadge communicated with Brewster, who had a direct line to General Washington. The young major decided it was time to prepare Woodhull for duty. On October 29, Scott officially resigned his position as head of the spy network, giving command to Tallmadge. The ambitious major finally had the chance to put his radical ideas into action.

*   *   *

Benjamin Tallmadge, Caleb Brewster and Abraham Woodhull were old friends, each of them having grown up in Setauket, Long Island. Brewster and Woodhull made a strange pair. Woodhull was quiet, polite and mild-mannered. Other than a brief stint in a local militia, he didn't seek out military service. Born into a family of humble farmers, he saw the life of a farmer as his destiny. However, the death of his relative, Nathanial Woodhull, at the Battle of New York galvanized his anti-British feelings. But for that event, Woodhull the farmer might have kept on farming undisturbed. Brewster loved action. He had no bone to pick with British. His motivations may have been childish, but his natural talents could not be ignored. Together, the three of them formed the nucleus of the Culper Ring. Tallmadge was the "idea" man and ringleader; Brewster and Woodhull ("Culper") served as de facto deputies.

Setauket was a close-knit community and a strong-hold of rebel sympathizers. Everyone knew every-one else, and many people were related. Brewster and Woodhull shared a common ancestor several generations back. This network of family and neighborly alliances made the success of the Culper Ring possible. Agents trusted no one outside of well-established friends of the rebellion. Only Tallmadge was entrusted with relaying intelligence back to Washington. This faithfulness to protocol prevented discovery of the spy ring for the remain-der of the war. Woodhull was probably the most cautious of all, sticking religiously to his alias and insisting that his letters be destroyed. At first he even resisted the idea of using the written word, preferring instead that all communications be ver-bal. He was soon convinced of the impracticality of that idea.

Tallmadge's first job was to restore Woodhull to a level of "respectability" in his community. He had been captured and held in rebel territory for some time. His reappearance would seem suspicious. The British had recently stated that anyone disavowing Congress and swearing allegiance to the Crown would be pardoned at the end of the war. So, Woodhull made that declaration, and his Loyalist neighbors had restored faith in him. They never once suspected him of anything underhanded.

In late October 1778, Woodhull wrote his first of many "Samuel Culper" letters. Not having a Yale education, his spelling and punctuation are less than perfect, and his style in somewhat meandering. However, he does eventually get down to detail. His writing becomes tighter and cleaner with time, as well. In the first months of the Culper Ring's activities, Woodhull had by far the most dangerous work. He had to regularly make the 55-mile trip down the Long Island road into the city. This meant leaving his elderly parents behind and running the risk of capture. Marauders and British patrols were all over the roads. Woodhull hated this part of his work, but understood its necessity. At the Brooklyn ferry, he had to purchase a two-shilling permit. He no doubt raised some suspicions among the guards: What was a Long Island farmer doing all the way down there with no produce to trade? Not for the first time, Woodhull stressed to his superiors the importance of destroying all of his letters. Fortunately for later generations, Washington's staff did not destroy the letters.

Washington was pleased with the work of Woodhull. As for the intelligence delivered, he was especially curious about the British supply chain. Heavy stockpiling would indicate an offensive campaign in the spring. The British clearly understood their delicate situation. New York was totally reliant on the outside world. A few ships lost at sea might result in disaster.

On one of his last trips into the city, Woodhull made a connection with someone he could trust: his brother-in-law, Amos Underhilll. With this connection, Woodhull had someone on the inside of British territory, able to keep a daily watch on the comings and goings of the redcoats. Underhill was a merchant whose family was struggling with financial burdens. He was eager to do anything within his power to undermine the British occupiers. Underhill was one of less than 5,000 true civilians who had remained in the city since its takeover. In the summer of 1778, there were approximately 9,000 British soldiers and support personnel in the city. Underhill was the first true "inside" agent of the Culper Ring, and his dispatches would be particularly influential for the rebel cause.

*   *   *

The nucleus of the Culper Ring was strong, but the peripheral agents were not quite meeting expectations. Brewster typically recruited off-duty sailors and soldiers as messengers and go-betweens, a tactic that was not sustainable in the long run. These agents couldn't be full trusted not to blab about their activities. Likewise, they didn't truly owe their allegiance to Brewster or Tallmadge. The ringleaders, therefore, held a meeting to discuss their shared problem.

"We need civilian agents, like Woodhull, who work for us only," said Brewster.

"I fully agree, but the recruiting of people for such dangerous work will not be easy. And when money is the only motivator, the quality of the intelligence no doubt suffers."

"I have a possible solution. We give small, simple tasks to most of our agents. No individual will be able to see the whole picture, and no individual is too much in harm's way. At least within reason. We have the means to offer fair salaries and some degree of protection. What do you say?"

"In theory it sounds agreeable. If we could just find a dozen more men like Abraham Woodhull, we could win this war. But the man is one of a kind," observed Tallmadge.

"He is that. He's also more cautious than a pet cat. I worry sometimes that his caution goes too far and restricts his usefulness."

"Better a cautious agent than a dead agent."

"Well," said Brewster, "I can't argue with that. Did you read his most recent report, the one containing the extremely precise troop numbers? Imagine the enormous strides we could achieve with more than one agent doing just that level of work. Even Washington said he was doing a capital job."

Tallmadge shook his head in agreement. "The only thing that's hampering us, really, is the slow transit of the information. Accurate intelligence is useless if it's not delivered in time. Woodhull's extreme caution and unwillingness to trust anyone else has brought things to a slow pace. Too slow. More agents in the field would certainly solve all of our problems. Let me think: I made the acquaintance of several people last year who may just be able to help us with this business."

CHAPTER 6: TOOLS OF THE TRADE

The Culper Ring didn't refer to themselves as spies. Instead, they talked about their "job" or their "business." The shame of being a spy was a powerful stigma. Not just a spy, but a spy paid for his work, was the lowest of the low. For that reason, Abraham Woodhull refused a salary, insisting only that his expenses be reimbursed, and he be granted a small per diem. He told his associates that he was serving the "Cause of Liberty" and not simply being a mercenary. In his memoir, he barely mentioned his work during the war.

The winter of 1778 – 79 was spent streamlining the chain of communication between Manhattan and General Washington's headquarters. With Underhill's lodgings as a convenient base of operations, both Underhill and Woodhull were able to collect copious amounts of information within the city, all without raising suspicion. Once that information made it to Setauket, Brewster's agents took it across the Sound. On the Connecticut, a chain of agents carried letters on to Tallmadge. The weakest link in this whole chain was the trip from Manhattan to Setauket. The road was 55 miles long and incredibly dangerous.

Jonas Hawkins and Austin Roe were among the first new recruits to the ring. They took turns carrying messages from Manhattan to Setauket. Both of them were natives to Setauket, and, therefore, Tallmadge and his crew entirely trusted them. They shared a common upbringing and dislike of the British. Adding these men to the network immediately boosted its efficiency. In January 1779, a letter made it from Woodhull to General Washington in less than a week, an astounding accomplishment given the geography, climate, and dangers of the route. Each member of the ring had a convincing cover story in the event of questioning or capture.

With the help of his brother-in-law, Woodhull had a much easier time gathering information on the

British. His longest letter to Washington was seven pages, full of details about deployment, provisions, and troop numbers. One of the first critical pieces of intelligence that the ring uncovered was the build-up of "privateer" vessels -- essentially pirates working on behalf of the British navy. Brewster and Woodhull both saw evidence of this build-up and dutifully reported the news to headquarters. Even the British commander, Sir Henry Clinton, had visited the shipyards, evidence that something was afoot. Washington and Tallmadge puzzled over this intelligence, not knowing quite what to make of it.

"It looks to me, sir, that the British intend a Connecticut invasion come summer. The fleet is being built on the Sound side of the island. Where else would they be going?" asked Tallmadge.

Washington had learned about the wiliness of the British general first-hand. He'd been bested on the field more than once, and was understandably wary. "The thing is, Benjamin, I see no strategic advantage in Connecticut. If they intend such a landing, surely it must be a diversion. It's been all too easy to learn of these happenings. My instinct tells me something is not quite right here. We need more information."

"Sir, our network of agents has become much more efficient than we could have hoped, but still there are unavoidable delays. A lame horse, foul weather, a curious British guard ... These and any number of other things slow our progress. I'd like your permission to investigate a new method of delivery."

"I won't oppose it," Washington said, "but remember this: We cannot let the flow of intelligence be disrupted, not even for a moment."

"Certainly not. I have another idea, as well. Presently our messages are written in black ink. I would like to ferret out a way to make the ink invisible; this may well protect the lives of our agents should they be searched."

Fortunately for Tallmadge, Sir James Jay had recently developed one of the world's first invisible inks. Jay called his invention "sympathetic" ink. When used with ordinary white paper, the ink left no trace. A second chemical applied to the paper rendered the writing visible again. James' brother John undertook the manufacture of these chemicals, which wasn't easy. The process was delicate and expensive. Washington was ready to spare no expense, however, as the incredible ink would offer greater security and peace of mind for the Culper Ring's field agents.

Prior to Jay's invisible ink, the only such inks were organic in nature, such as lemon juice or vinegar.

Heat alone was the only tool needed to make the ink legible. This made them poor alternatives. Another popular method of communication involved the transmission of messages in parts. One part consisted of a "fake" message. The second part was called the "grille" and was a blank paper with portions cut out. When the grille was laid over the fake message, the actual message appeared. The trouble in this method was that two separate pieces had to be delivered separately, greatly increasing the odds of miscommunication.

Although it was costly and difficult to produce at first, the Culper Ring eventually had a healthy supply of this new ink. The British would never manage to unravel its chemical secrets. What's more, is that the agents could write on virtually anything -- books, maps, margins of newspapers -- and so not arouse suspicion by carrying seemingly blank sheets of paper.

*   *   *

By the spring of 1779, Washington was once more eager to augment the stream of information leaking out of New York. He had unsuccessfully propositioned Lewis Pintard, an American commissary stationed in the city for the care of prisoners, to deliver intelligence from the British headquarters. Somehow, word of this request had gotten out, putting Pintard in a tight situation. He angrily refused. Washington's next choice was a native by the name of George Higday.

Everything came to a halt on July 2, when a surprise attack threw the whole operation into jeopardy. Tallmadge's camp was attacked in the pre-dawn hours by a force of two hundred highly skilled British soldiers. Eight of Tallmadge's men were taken prisoner, along with the captain's horse. The horse's saddlebags contained a letter discussing George Higday, including the location of his residence. The captain was dumbfounded as to how the British knew where to find him. The troops had seemed to target his group specifically. He didn't know that a month earlier the British had seized a letter written in black ink that mentioned both the spy ring and something about a secret new liquid. The letter was intended for Tallmadge. Consequently, the British decided they had better capture Tallmadge and extract more information if possible. Washington maintained calm, but wanted no repeat performance of this blunder. Mostly he was concerned for the safety of Higday. British troopers arrested him on July 13, and he offered his confession. Clinton was not a vindictive commander, and let Higday return home. He was, of course, useless to Washington at that point. The worry now for the rebels was how seriously the British were investigating the existence of a "Culper" in their midst.

They certainly had tagged Tallmadge as commander of the ring. The agents would have to be more careful than ever before.

*   *   *

Invisible ink wasn't the only method that the Culper Ring used to relay messages. For some time, Tallmadge had experimented with the development of a unassuming but hopefully hard-to-crack cipher. In Europe, cryptography was a highly advanced practice. However, no one in the Culper Ring had the linguistic or mathematical background to invent an entirely new cipher. Even if an expert could be brought in as a consultant, there was of course the problem of how to adequately train everyone in the network. Fortunately, the British also were not expecting any level of sophistication in terms of coded messages. Tallmadge settled on a one-to-one numeric substitution technique that was a favorite of John Adams. He composed what's known as a "Code Dictionary," with numbers assigned to common names, places and frequently used words. As an example, George Washington was "711" and Setauket was "20." Tallmadge also included additional symbols to signify verb tenses. The code was remarkable for someone not trained in cryptography. An intercepted letter was now less of a concern, as the contents would be an unreadable mishmash of letters and numbers. Tallmadge's code did its job: It was unsophisticated enough for all of his agents to create and decipher, while complicated enough to avoid deciphering by ordinary British soldiers.

CHAPTER 7: A NEW INSIDE MAN

Abraham Woodhull, never having the stoutest nerves, was beginning to crack under the pressure of traveling back and forth between New York and Setauket. In April 1779, he was mugged by privateers along the road. In May, during a trip into the city, his home was raided and his father beaten by a British commander, John Simcoe. Woodhull had begun once more to arouse suspicion. He wanted more to gain some safe distance from the spy game. Even when he wasn't feeling paranoid, he had the strong impression that he didn't fit in with the likes

of Benjamin Tallmadge, and certainly not with
General Washington. His discussions with Tallmadge revealed a frightened, severely anxious state
of mind.

"I'm telling you, it's become too dangerous for me
to travel this road. People begin to wonder openly
what my business honestly is."

"Look, Abraham," began Tallmadge, "we, too, think
of your safety. General Washington remarks again
and again how valuable you have been to the cause.
If you think it's time for you to remove yourself,
well, that's a decision that I have to leave up to
you."

"Then I think it's time. I've made a close friendship
with a fellow patriot who stays with my kinsman
Mr. Underhill. His temperament is uniquely suited
to this line of work. I can vouch for him without
hesitation."

"I'd like to hear more," said Tallmadge.

Woodhull gasped slightly. "Surely you understand
the need for secrecy. I would much prefer we main-
tain absolute silence on the issue of identity. For
now, we can refer to this agent as 'Samuel Culper,
Jr.'"

Tallmadge was amused. His nervous and perhaps too-cautious friend had given birth to a "son" in the spy game. Still, he had absolute faith that if Woodhull vouched for someone, that was a statement to take seriously.

*   *   *

In his code dictionary, this new agent received the designation "723." His real name was Robert Townsend. He was an extraordinary figure, and quite unlike his fellows in the Culper Ring. Townsend came from Oyster Bay, much closer to the city than Setauket. He had a mixed background, and owed some amount of allegiance to Quaker and Episcopalian heritages. He nurtured an idealist point of view, but still approached the world in a practical way. He was vulnerable to melancholy, and remained a bachelor his whole life. Also unlike the other members of the ring, he never actually took up arms during the war. He had previously served in a peacetime militia under General Nathanial Woodhull. Townsend and the elder Woodhull struck up a fast friendship, and quickly gauged each other's Patriot tendencies. When Woodhull proposed a way for Townsend to serve his country without firing a musket, he jumped at the chance.

Townsend descended from Quakers and so had no strong political allegiance, at least not until the

outbreak of war. His father was a known Whig (patriot) and was nearly imprisoned when the British
took Long Island in 1776. After swearing allegiance
to the king, neither Robert nor his father was harassed again. Following in the footsteps of other
Townsends, Robert went into business for himself
in Manhattan. He set up a dry-goods store that
catered to the British military. He also invested in
other businesses, such as a coffeehouse. He did extremely well both during and after the war. Being
well known and liked by British commanders, he
was a perfect choice for Tallmadge's Culper Ring.
No one would blink an eye if he traveled frequently: He was a businessman, after all.

The impetus for Townsend to ally himself secretly
with the rebel cause was none other than Thomas
Paine's famous pamphlet, "Common Sense." Paine
accused the Quaker leadership of kowtowing to the
British and abandoning the founding principles of
their faith. Townsend was spellbound by Paine's
rhetoric. He still held fast to the nonviolent aspects
of Quaker belief. However, intellectually, he had
come over to the side of the rebellion. Espionage
on behalf of the Continental Army represented a
way to show allegiance to the revolution without
actually taking up arms. Another strong motivator
for Townsend was the treatment of Loyalist citizens
on Long Island. Rather than being rewarded for
their faithfulness, residents were placed under mar-

tial law and constantly harassed. A once-friendly local population was becoming bitter, to the dismay of British commanders. In his travels, Townsend no doubt heard these grumblings. By 1779, he was ready to turn his back on England. He only needed a way out. Woodhull certainly sensed this and provided just such an outlet.

*   *   *

William Tyron launched a vicious attack on the Connecticut shores in July 1779. Villages were burned and thousands of dollars worth of loot was taken. The local militias were no match for the heavily armed British regulars. The attack itself was diversionary, part of a plan to draw Washington away from his defensive position and then surprise him in the open field. The plan was well conceived, but failed for two reasons. First, the Culper Ring had previously noted the buildup of ships. On July 7, Washington received further confirmation from the spy network that an attack was imminent, but that it was only a ruse. Wisely, the commander-in-chief held his forces back. The terrible fate of the coastal residents was sealed, but the Revolution remained intact. The second reason for the failure was that General Clinton had abandoned the plan after it had begun. Perhaps he saw that Washington had not taken the bait. In the end, the attacks were strategically irrelevant.

Meanwhile, Woodhull (Culper, Sr.) was busily training Townsend (Culper, Jr.) in the ways of spycraft
and secrecy. In several letters, he expressed admira-
tion for the intelligence and hard work undertaken
by his trainee. Townsend was quick to offer a return on investment: He identified a Loyalist double
agent working behind rebel lines.

The Culper Ring was slowly perfecting its craft.
Townsend kept his business interests running
smoothly while performing espionage on the side.
This prevented any suspicion from falling upon
him. Woodhull for the most part stayed in Setauket. Hawkins, one of the original messengers,
retired from the business, leaving only Roe to travel
between New York and Setauket. The ring avoided
in-person meetings, preferring instead to use "dead
drops," secret locations for plating messages. These
dead drops were often small holes hidden in open
fields or in the woods. It was about this time that
an intriguing new member jointed the Culper Ring,
a woman by the name of Anna Strong.

$*$ $*$ $*$

Agent 355 (the code number means "lady") was
married to a prominent Whig who was currently
imprisoned on one of the infamous prison ships.
She had more than enough reason to hate the
British. As a neighbor of Amos Underhill, Anna

Strong eventually came within the sphere of Woodhull and Townsend. One of Strong's main duties was to pose as the wife of Woodhull. Single men were suspicious, but a married man traveling with his wife couldn't possibly be a spy. It was risky work, but Woodhull was impressed by his comrade's fortitude.

In September of 1799, Captain Nathan Woodhull (Abraham's uncle) also entered the service of the Culper Ring on a part-time basis. The captain was a member of the Loyalist militia, so converting to the side of the rebels was a massive win. Both he and 355 worked on this basis, which was believed to arouse less suspicion from the British occupiers.

As the winter of 1799 approached, the British appeared willing and able to hunker down for another season in New York. A French attack on the city never materialized, and the British had more than enough provisions, firewood and hay. The war would drag on for another year, at least. During the winter, Townsend made an significant discovery while he rubbed elbows with British officers. He uncovered he plan to devalue the Continental currency by flooding the market with counterfeits. Congress upended that plan by recalling all their bills and declaring bankruptcy.

CHAPTER 8: TWILIGHT OF THE RING

Beginning in 1780, the Culper Ring would gradually come apart. There were several reasons for this. First, both Woodhull's and Townsend's fears of discovery hampered their efforts. Townsend flatly refused to put anything into writing after one of his agents -- a cousin -- was stopped by rebels and nearly came to an unlucky end. Woodhull refused to make the trip into New York anymore. The regular courier, Roe, had become wary of increased British troop numbers and stepped-up patrols. Indeed, as the British were elsewhere losing ground, the number of Her Majesty's troops stationed in the city grew. The concentration of British forces in one location had the effect of making intelligence gathering somewhat less influential. For Tallmadge and Washington, they both became more occupied with purely military matters.

Serious negotiations for peace began in 1782. Fighting wars on several continents was becoming unsustainable to the British. They had become reconciled to the thought of losing the American colonies. The last official "Culper Letter" was sent on February 21, 1783. Although Woodhull was admired for his diligence, his intelligence reports were no longer necessary. Peace was clearly around the corner.

*   *   *

Upon the conclusion of the war, the members of the Culper Ring settled back into "ordinary" life. For the most part, they had little to say about their activities, even many years after the conclusion of the events. There was still a powerful stigma associated with spying. Autobiographies and memoirs of the members either don't mention their work during the war, or provide an alternate version of events. Indeed, the Culper Ring was unknown to historians for more than a century. Today we understand that this small network of brave civilians and soldiers may have been the difference between winning and losing the War for Independence.